FROM THE TRICKSTER SCRIBE
PUBLISHING POETRY COLLECTION:

Bitter Witch

And Other Pet Names

BY MJE CLUBB

Imprint: Trickster Scribe Publishing 2023

The story, all names, characters, and incidents portrayed in this production are fictitious. No identification with actual persons (living or deceased), places, buildings, and products are intended, nor should be inferred.

Paperback ISBN 978-1-962673-21-1

Cover art: MJE Clubb 2022
Illustrations: MJE Clubb 202

Third Edition [2025]

Bibliographical note:
"Bitter Witch and Other Pet Names" was first published in 2023. This is the Third Edition of "Bitter Witch and Other Pet Names" with an updated cover, title page art, illustrations, and ISBN.

Dedication...

Thank-you to my husband Jeremy for sharing a friendship with me no matter what our personal situations were. You are truly a one-of-a-kind man, and the only person I could ever consider spending my life with.

In the words of Chrissy Amphlett: *"You're the sun who makes me shine / When you're around, I'm always laughing."*

As your wife and friend, I promise to love and care for you, to be worthy of your love, to always be honest with you, kind, patient, and forgiving until my last breath.

Also, a nostalgic thank-you to my father who created such a "bitter witch". I literally could have not become who I am today without your intervention.

MJE Clubb
Oregon, USA
March 2023

Daughter

I held you in my arms,
And saw my mother in your face.
Did you feel the panic?
The momentary clench of muscle?
This was the reward for fifteen hours of labor?

It was not your fault.
It was never your fault.

With age, you became your father,
But only in your face.
The bitterness each time I recognized him.
The ache of memories.
It had never been your hands on my throat.

It was not your fault.
It was never your fault.

My nose is barely above your crown.
Maybe it's not anymore.
The time keeps whipping away from me, from us...
You are so clearly you.
A delight!

Forgive me.
Forgive me.

Liminal Youngest

I am the liminal youngest.
Last of four, but not last of five;
Yet still the last.

Does anyone else remember the blue skirt?
The little colored sweater I wore?
Even though it was summer...

A restless daughter, in the heat;
Forced to stand still.
Look at all of us standing, so somber.

Smothering inappropriate laughter;
Because I'm not the youngest.
Yet, I still am.

The barrier between four and five,
Is an aluminum plate stamped into the dirt,
At a church on the hill.

Earthen

If I die today,
Plant a pine tree on my grave.
For I will miss you,
And yearn patiently for you,
Until we meet again in the earth.

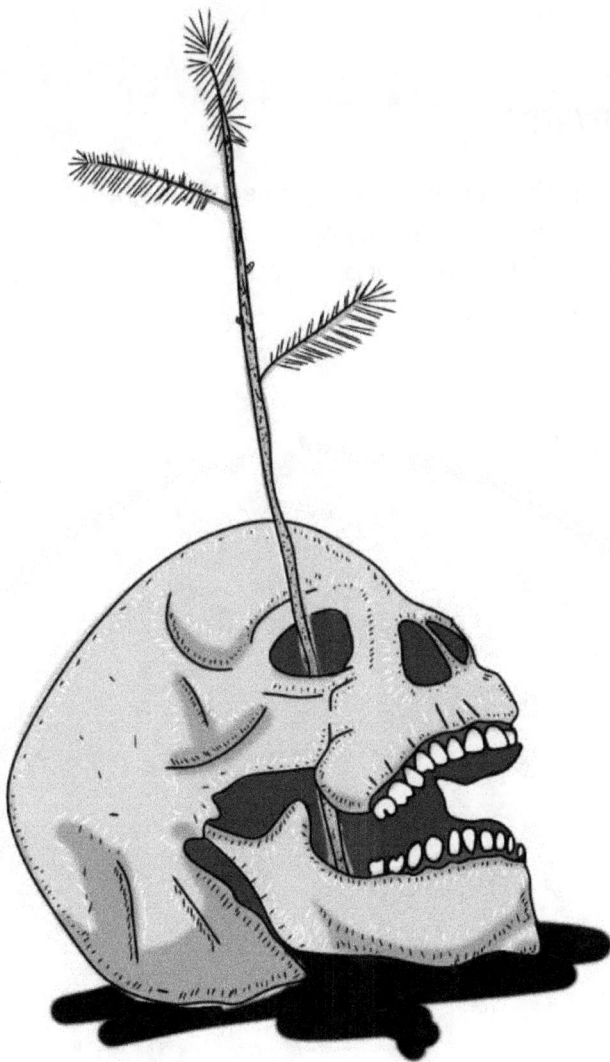

Coyotes I

In childhood keening songs filled the night;
Reassuring, and horrifying.
Knowing I wasn't alone, but also
I wasn't alone.

Ape Caves

In the darkness of the caves is a trail.
Fallen boulders squeeze and crowd us,
Stacked precariously to the ceiling.
Our lamps seem so piteously feeble here.
The unknown yawns before us.

My faith in the path wavered,
I could feel the tons of stone,
Darkness hanging over my head,
Like a silent, smothering guillotine.
The path itself seems untrustworthy.

Your fingers found mine,
Gently squeezing warmth back in.
"Just a little bit farther, keep going."
When I faltered, "we got this."
Anxiety loosens on my throat.

Dimly, and then brightly,
A beam of sunshine appeared ahead.
The metal ladder was filthy, but strong.
It held us, and yielded us to the light.
Just as you knew it would.

Forgotten

A moment is ephemeral poetry.
Something to be appreciated but not held,
Just a beautiful transition.
I wonder how much poetry I have forgotten...

Clouds and Lovers

Even in the milky light of the clouds,
You glow.
That is not to say you emanate light—
You are the light.
Is this what love is?

Cheating

Is poetry cheating? I ask.
Shouldn't I be following rules?

There is silence.

It is only a betrayal to not write at all,
I whisper to myself and type.

Red Flags

It always seemed like a character flaw—
To me—
That men should hate felines,
In the same breath,
That they compare cats to women.

Familial Love

They love each other very much—
I saw it as a child.

In their embraces,
Mutual empathy and kindness.

In the way they dreamed together.
It overflowed.

I just never understood,
Why there wasn't any left for me.

Nightmares

When I was a child,
Nightmares visited each night.
The dread of death haunted my sleep.
The horror was my constant companion.

Now I am an adult,
And the nightmares are gone.
Now I find myself,
Terribly alone.

Gone Soft

Myself as a teen was always ready to fight:
My body was lean,
My hands calloused and clenched.
Quick with the knife and machete.
Quiet and always on edge.

Myself in my mid-thirties is different:
My body is soft,
My hands open and gentled.
Quick to laugh with the absurdity.
Quiet still, but more empathetic.

I miss the physicality of my youth...
But in return, I've turned into someone,
Who would have protected the teen.

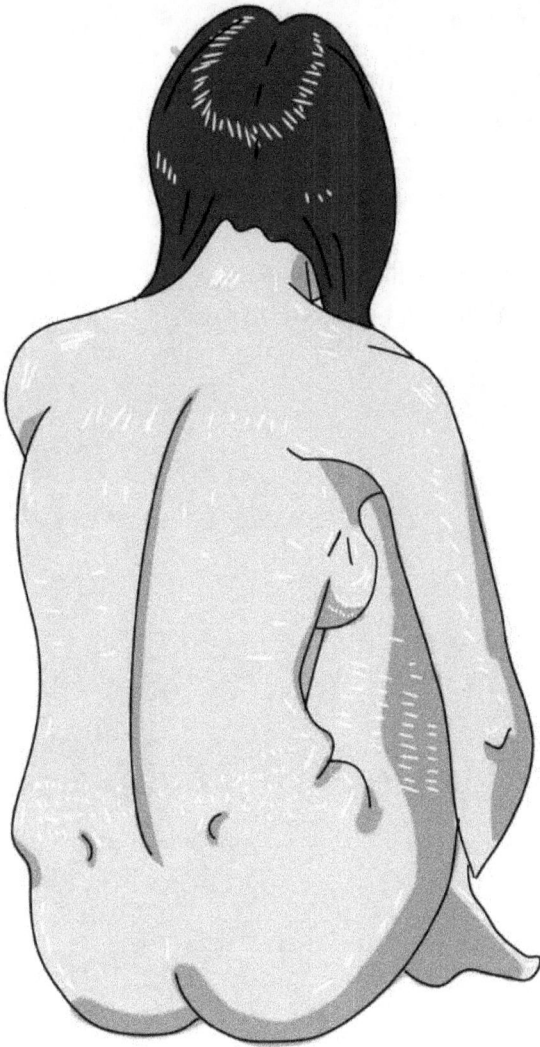

Fifteen

My daughter at fifteen,
is so unlike myself at fifteen.

I can't help but wonder...

Would she have liked that skinny,
Wretched girl that used to be me?

First Husband

Calling him "my first husband",
Sounds as if he were deceased.

I assure you; he was never dead.

The only thing that was killed,
Was our mutual love.

And he killed that himself.

Narcissus

October:

Soil crusted under my nails as
I buried them in the dark cold earth.
Casually, I returned to the site often.
Without fanfare, they disappeared.
And no witnesses could be found,
Other than myself.

February:

Surely now the end of winter is near...
The burial sites still seem naked,
Noticeable, like a neon sign.
Gripped, I put my eye to the earth,
And scan closely for evidence of my actions.
Lo, green fingers of growth push to the sun.

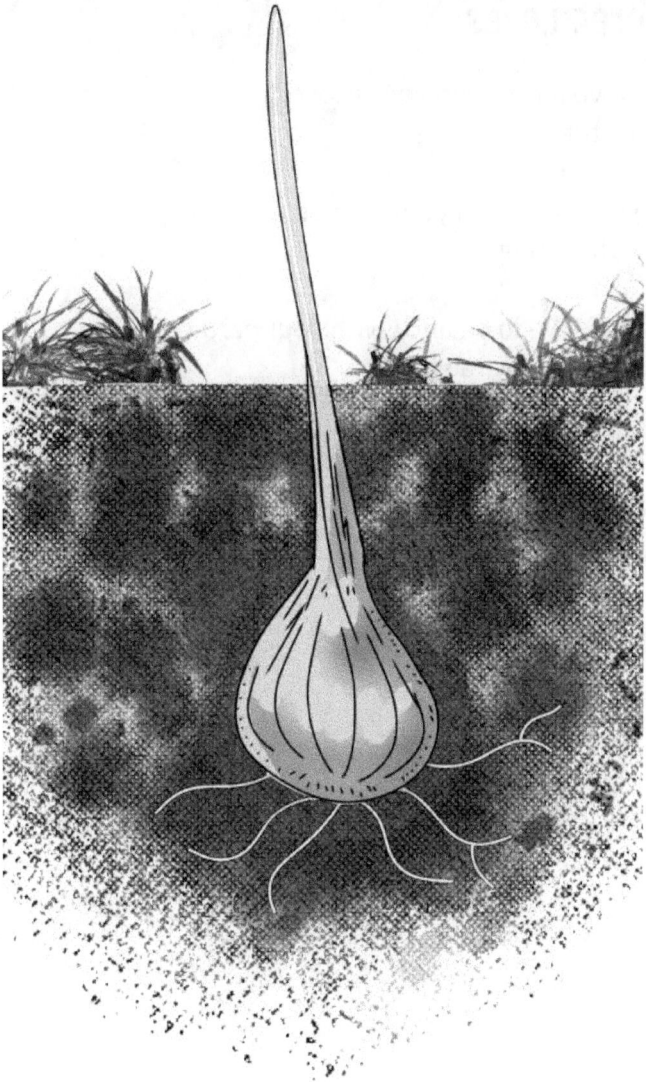

Three Loves

To love more than you're loved,
Is torture.

To love less than you're loved,
Is suffocating.

But to love in balance with your partner...
Feels incomparable.

A Sixteenth Cherokee

My mother said she was a sixteenth Cherokee.
My father said he was a sixteenth of a forgotten
tribe.
With the understanding of a child,
Math predicted I must be a sixteenth native as well.
I delighted in the story.

As an adult I looked deeper and took tests,
To become empty-handed.
Then I realized, like many other white families,
It must have been a lie we told ourselves.
To assuage guilt.

Curls of a Mother

In the mirror, I see her hair.
My unwilling inheritance.

I dye it, fry it, flatten it into submission.
Consequently I don't see her each time I look.

It works mostly—except when it doesn't.
Her visage haunted my periphery.

Used to.

Recently I've stopped the processes.
No longer fighting what I see...

I lean into the curls and the gleaming
Silver strands tucked throughout.

I look and force away the old intrusive idea.
Now the reflection only shows me.

Usually.

Grippers

I am young, I tend to think.

But then there are moments
Like when my children point to my feet
And say confidently:
"Grippers"

What the fuck.

A Summoning Spell

If you stare into the mirror and say:
Bloody Mary
Bloody Mary
Bloody Mary
She will appear and consume you.

Knowing this, I stare into the mirror and say:
I Love You
I Love You
I Love You
And wait.

Middle of Ages

Stuck in the middle of ages,
I'm lost in a sea of mundanity.
Somehow too old and young to be respected.

I was too young
To appreciate being the youngest
In the whole world.

And I fear I will die
Long before I reach
The oldest.

Bitter Witch and Other Pet Names

My ex-husband says: *Social Justice Warrior.*
Like it is a fantasy role-play subclass.
He meant it as an insult,
But that barb rolled off my armor class.

Men have called me: *bitchy, bossy, slut.*
But had I been a man,
They would be lauding me instead.
The inconsistency seems obvious to me.

My father called me: *a Bitter Witch,*
For condemning internment camps.
In the same breath, he said "I love you."
I think I am too much of him, for his liking.

My derby sisters call me: *Lulu*
Because it was easier than C'thu Lulu
The name I gave myself,
To feel untouchable and strong.

My lover calls me: *My love, honey, babe.*
Not because he's forgotten my name,
But because in my husband's heart,
I touch so many places.

My offspring calls me: *mom.*
At times it will be "Muriel" playfully,

And pretend I hate it from her.
Though I don't—I can still hear her love

The latter two seem to have it right.

Sometimes I am a Fish

Not because I swim well,
I could not swim until adulthood.

But because when I have hiccups,
I tell myself confidently:

I am NOT a fish!
And the hiccups dissipate.

It almost always works.
Almost.

The Curse

In anger she cursed me:
I hope you get a child who treats you
Just as badly as you treat me!
She said with venom.

Now I am grown and birthed that child.
The threat has come to fruition...
I never knew it would be like this:
She's a delight.

Dusting Off

I looked upon the shambles of my life:
My trampled heart,
My aching soul,
My tears exhausted and
My willpower dimmed.
Then I croak to myself:
Opportunity.

Stormy Weather

I raised my face to the sky, expecting the chill.

The weather was temperamental like a man:
Making its own self-important chaos
And indecision
Everyone else's problem.

I had endured worse.

Disbelief

You stand there,
To tell me that milk
doesn't grow on trees.
Then,
In the same breath,
Have me shake the branches
For a cow.

Totally Normal High School Things

Peers stealing referral slips to slut-shame
By plastering them on my locker.

Having my locker broken into
And someone put a cow femur inside.

Driving to school in the morning
And being slapped in the face by my mom.

Seventeen and moving out at midnight
Taking a couple boxes--my entire life--with me.

Crying all day in the school bathrooms
Heartbroken and getting good grades.

Wanting to be loved by anyone
And finding nothing at home or school.

There was, however, some really tasty
Pizza and chocolate milk.

Nineteen-Ninety-Six

In 1996 the world sank beneath a deluge of rain.
Brown water turned our homes into islands.

My father took us out in an old row boat
Into the expanse, and I could not swim.

Just a child clinging to the aluminum seat.

The waters receded, revealing strange gifts
From the flood to my father's property.

A doghouse, stranded on our muddy road.
Random items reallocated from other families.

Worst of all were the large, marooned fish.
The vanishing water left them crazed.

Fish charged at me from the puddles,
I wasn't in danger physically, but

--their madness still haunts me.

Humility

~~Knwoing~~ the right word is powerful
Knowing ~~teh rihgt~~ word is powerful
~~Knwoing~~ the
Knowing ~~teh~~
~~teh~~

Fuck it.

As of yet, Unknown

Do you really want to be known
For this? They ask.

Did you mean:
Do you really want to be known?

Mind the Gap

The generational gap
Only extends so far as
To prevent me from feeling
Anything but disgust
Toward women desperate
For the approval of
Unworthy men.

A Kindness of Wounds

Overnights and over years
I found my best friend.

Struggle had tainted our lives,
And given us some kinship.

My wounds created a coldness and walls;
Hers had given her empathy and kindness.

I will gladly surround myself
By my betters, like her.

Ancient Interwebs

Wondrously, I saw the internet blossom
With the same eyes
That watched predators find me,
At thirteen, online.

Free AOL CDs were cool though.

Anthropology

Loving anthropology reminds me
That maybe we were always like this.

Thus, I stare at bones and pottery,
To feel less alone in my soul.

An Afternoon in October

We're waiting on you, he called down
From top-deck to mid-deck.

Me: *Are you sure? It's a little late,*
But you could still change your mind...

A smile played on his face, *come up*.
Beaming, I joined him.

Gratitude

Sitting on the couch
In a clean, warm, well-lit room
I am warm, safe, and loved.

Silently, unnoticed, I cry there.
I know that this is exactly
Everything I ever wanted.

Future Ghost

Will the ghost that haunts my wet bones
Stick around when my skeleton has dried?

Will my books miss me
When my fingers no longer caress them?

Once I'm gone, will anyone notice?
Maybe that doesn't matter. Maybe.

Less Than a Dozen

I am a shadow of what was wanted.
Those who came before me.
They played the roles right:
Strong or perfect, smart or loyal;
And then there is just me.

When the eldest had children,
My mother traveled to visit
Constantly throughout each week and year.
She was so extremely involved;
And I expected the same.

But when I had my child,
The differences were vast.
I did so much alone, only the eldest
Came visited and helped,
In all the ways she had been helped.

There was no interest in me, or my child...
Less than a dozen times--
That's how often they met her.
The only effort I consistently see,
Is the guilt they try to place on me, for their actions.

Attention to Detail

I knew each foot fall like a fingerprint,
Every sigh was the change in wind.

I could see the fine different hue of blue
In eyes of either placid lake or stormy sky.

How loudly was that door shut?
Did the plate sit in the sink or crash?
When was silence too much silence?

Stepping on eggshells with bare feet
I begged my soles not to bleed.

Sanguineous remnants only led to anger,
And, poor as I was, I couldn't afford that.

I got very good at hearing diminutive details,
Even as my vocal prowess decayed.
Those who recognize this feeling, know what's
unspoken.

Self-Inflicted Crimes

In many ways I borrow from tomorrow,
I steal sleep like a thief,
Bargaining for more time that I will not have,
Just to get through today.

I will run out of *self* to mortgage.
Eventually.

... Once more couldn't hurt.

Handfuls

Looking at my child who is mortified
Having broken something of mine
I hold in my hands two things:
What my parents taught me to say,
And what I've learned to say instead.
I choose the latter.

A Study in Love

Staring down at my soft flesh,
Tiger-striped with stretch marks,
Pocked from picking on myself,
Veins on my pale thighs,
Lines under mossy eyes...
It is a wonder that I manage, somehow,
To not love myself.

Loving Realization

There was a moment when everything,
Snapped into place, giving me clarity.

I was talking you up, to my friend,
When it occurred to me,
I wanted to talk about you,
More than my last date.

And you held this glowing,
Place in my heart,
That no one could compare to.

Which is why whenever I saw,
That someone was mistreating you,
I would become so furious.

But somehow crossing state lines,
And getting away from my life,
Made me realize...

Oh shit.

I love you.

Reach into the Future

My palm grazes your cheek,
To reach beyond this moment in time.

Caressing the skin of the elderly man
You will be, even if I am not here.

Know that I love you and him unfalteringly.
And age never diminished the place you hold,
In my heart.

Willful Supplication

Gazing into the pools of silver and gold
I fall helplessly, incautiously, into the potential
Of spending every day in your embrace.

Let me yield into your beautiful arms:
The inverted night sky, complex and captivating
The universe scrolls across your skin.

Guide me, show me, move me,
In this choreographed bolero of ours
I lead, you lead, let's dance...

Take my willful supplication.

Struggle Within

Here I am, knowing it is an opportunity for more,
Even as I take a sledgehammer to my own knees.

A habit I've learned to do to myself, to get it done,
Before someone else can come along and do it for
me.

Relentlessly pulled down, an addict of self-
destruction.
I fall to the floor, hold my ribs, and shriek.

When will I stop this? When will I stop, stopping
myself?
Only soundless internal cries answer me.

The Restless Spirit

In the grim and haunted house called my soul,
Shadows are felt from the corners of my sight.

The stairs creak, the hairs raise behind my neck,
My skin prickles, and fists clench.

Concentrating, I focus on breathing.
Just to remind myself I survived.

Those older versions of myself, dark and angry,
Are only misty ghosts.

Terrible and frightening, but if I remember their nature,
Then they cannot grip me in the night.

I Beg You

Kiss the blood from my lips.

Steal the breath from my lungs.

Take the strength from my bones.

Let me crumble beneath you.

Coyotes II

I've promised myself to the coyotes, so...

When my mind is gone, and I am not myself,
Bathe me in a marinade and let me soak,
With a crown of fruit.

Lead me into the crisp desert, with the dry air,
That can suck the moisture from my lungs,
And let me lie in the sand.

When the agony of the sun becomes the chill of
night,
And the howls fill the air, starved for action,
I'll welcome the eager teeth of those puppies.

Let their mouths find the shell of my body,
That my mind has long since abandoned,
They'll return me to the cycle of the earth.

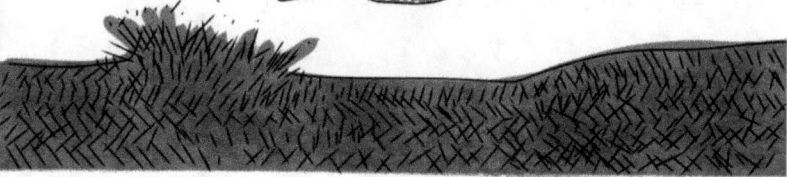

Sisterhood

Embrace and sing, my sister:

We are sisters,
We are sisters.

Born in strife and darkness...

We are sisters,
We are sisters.

The past is scarred across our souls,

We are sisters,
We are sisters.

Though I am younger, let me uplift you,

We are sisters,
We are sisters.

And bring you into the light to heal.

Feel It

Let me breathe in the cologne
Of woodsmoke and ice.
Fill my lungs so tightly,
That I cannot feel anything else—
Except this moment.

The bracing chill on my cheeks,
Shoulders quivering like the dead leaves,
In the breeze that catches my exhalation—
Like a flag in the wind and tears it apart.
Cold, seep into my bones.

Dancing tendrils of hair,
Caught by the unseen grasp of Boreas.
As the permafrost clutches my toes.
Numbness seeps into my calves,
Immobilizing my thighs.

Soundlessly, your hand grasps me,
And this is the warmest moment of my life.

Wallpaper

On my knees, scraping wallpaper from the wall,
Affords a chance for reflection.

On all the ways I had been hurt before,
And how I'm healing now.

I claw pieces away with my nails and ruminate
On my scars that no one can see.

This wall seems to stretch on forever when I am so close,
My work is not yet done.

Something was Amiss

"Greet me at the door when I come home."
Like a dog? I wonder.
Where is my greeting as I work over full-time,
And maintain the household?

"You are adequate."
Only adequate? I consider.
As I uplift you, build your confidence,
Surely a loved one should elicit more than this?

"Your presence makes me calm."
Like a blankie? I wince.
Everything about me, seems to be only:
How I can do things for you. Huh.

"I promise you I want that for us..."
But when? I ask.
Days and weeks and months turn into years,
Words seem hollow, as they echo off inaction.

"You should wear make-up when we go out."
Am I performing? I ponder.
How come I am the made-up dolly to play with,
Is the appearance more valuable than the human?

"I cannot wait six weeks!"
You never did, I remember.
My body was swollen, creating life!
While you played house without me.

"You deserve more than this."
This I said to myself, with hesitation.
Pushing away the clawing hands, reaching only to conquer.
I give myself a moment think of what I want instead.

Imposter?

What a fraud! I hiss to myself.
I sit at a desk, pretending to be an adult.
Feeling like I am suffering nearly enough,
Compared to everything I used to do.

I feel guilty for not suffering.
What is wrong with me?
I run my hands down my face.
Am I truly an imposter?

Or did I finally succeed?

Why can't I tell the difference?

Dark and Feral is She

Put this antlered crown upon my head.
Let it pierce and draw blood from thin skin.
Red rivers down my temples, pouring forth,
Matched to the flow gushing down my thighs.

Knowledge, Creation, Destruction, Wonder.

Goddess of the old ways, the animal, the soul.
Back to when fingers first clawed the earth.
Planting seeds, drinking the fermented waters,
And dreaming of the stars.

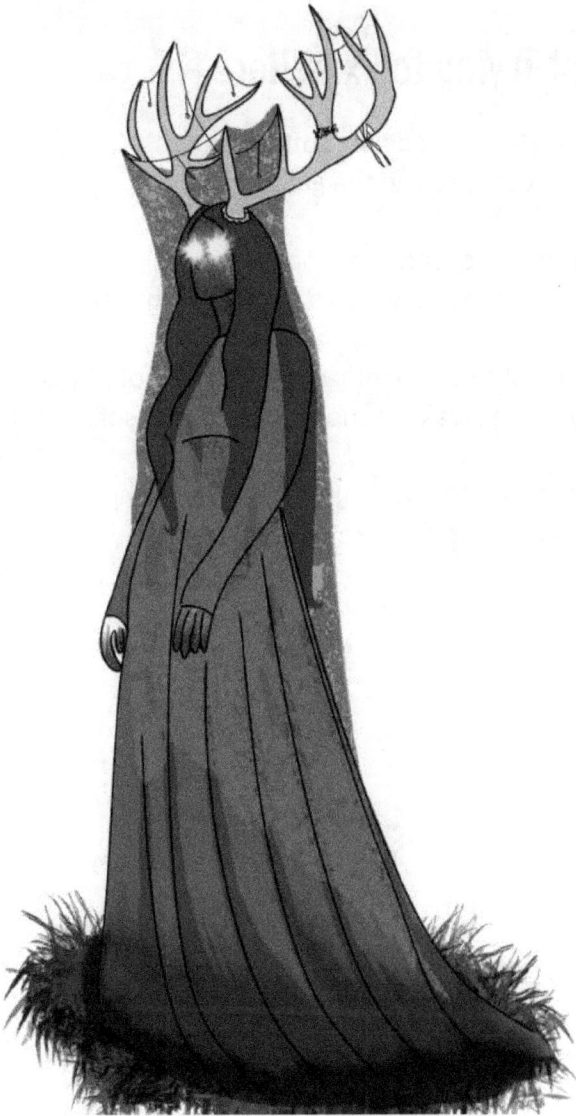

Just Trying to Exist Here

Let me lie in the dewy, soft moss.
Gaze at the stars in the galaxy.

Fall into love with the moon.
Allowing the misty fog to caress me into sleep.

Dream of the romantic entanglement of physics.
And when I wake in the golden rays of sol...

Hunch over the computer, join a meeting.
Press buttons, for fake paper money.

You're Thinking of Me

Maybe not today, I know,
Or even tomorrow, I'm sure.
But when you're grey with regret—

I know you will you think of me.
Your age-cracked lips will open to speak,
And only a croak of dust escapes.

Let each note of the songbird,
Cut you deeper than the last.
It's my grace gifted unto you.

I don't hope you die, obviously.
But I know in time you will perish,
A withered and unlovable man.

In years, I too will die. Like all mortals.
But I will live on freely in your mind.
A revenant curse that you suffer, eternally.

Not Just Me

It's complicated learning something new,
About someone who raised you,
Who had a profound impact on who you are...
And who you always knew didn't like you.

I don't know how to feel ...
Knowing it wasn't just me—
She never wanted any children.
My sister knew, did that hurt her more than I?

I cannot identify quite how to feel about it,
But it does make sense, in hindsight.
Maybe it's a relief, due to predetermination.
I never stood a chance. It wasn't my fault.

Stories in the Dark

In the wooden house, there were no lights,
Save for the industrious, ironclad woodstove,
That I would burn my legs on in the future.

The cracking glow of fires burned behind mesh,
Saving us from sparks, but not from all the smoke.
Glinting, apples covered in foil baked amid the
flames.

My tiny frame wedged into the chair with him,
And the moment felt filled with possibilities.
I was entranced by fire, and the rare delight of a
story.

He spun a tale that blended mystery, magic, and
adventure.
About magical horses that appeared during stormy
nights,
A brave and poor lad, and a girl trapped upon a glass
hill.

I would be well into adulthood, about twenty-five,
Before I heard another version about the glass-hill.
But, any other version was never as captivating as
that night.

I remember it so well, not because it was told so often,
No, I only clearly remember it being told once.
I remember it because that lone moment felt like love.

The Good, the Bad, and the Worst

Given the three sisters, they could be divided thusly:
The good
The bad
The worst

The good, the eldest, was the epitome of delight.
She got good grades, engaged in athletics,
Got married and gave birth to three children.
—please forget she ran away to break the cycle.

The bad, the middle, was the epitome of
industriousness.
She got good grades, engaged in her father's
interests.
She went to college and became like a second son.
—please forget she never left home and remained
alone.

The worst, the youngest, was the epitome of a
dreamer.
She got good grades and escaped into literature.
Got married, gave birth, got divorced and went to
college.
—please forget she ran away, got tattoos, and
continued to dream...

The Certainty of Knowing

My mother always knew,
how to share her grief well.
It was showing love that eluded her.

My father always knew,
When to hold his head up high,
That's how he looked down at me.

For me, I always knew,
That life was suffering,
But learned more with empathy.

Sorry Daughter

Wildfire and freezing storms.
Poisoned water and microplastics.
Nationalism and violence.
Guns but not healthcare.
Religiosity with severance of rights.
The bubble burst, and this is the debris...

I feel I should apologize to my daughter.

Nourishment

Pluck the caryopsis from the stalk,
Let the milk of wheat germ dribble into my mouth,
Ripened grain falling as rain upon my cheeks,
Gather it with cracked and dusty hands,
And grind them into a fine flour,
Rehydrate with yolk and fluids,
Let me put my love into the mix,
Work, knead, fold, and bake,
Eat from my efforts and scalded pan,
Prosper, and feel nourished my friends,
Join me, and sow the next generation,
Into the earth, our mother,
So we may eat together again.

No Afterlife

There is nothing beyond, I say.
"Isn't that depressing?"
"That's terrible, you're terrible for saying so."
"God will prove you wrong."

It is not terrible to me.
It means I can pour all my efforts into the now.
All my kindness and love spent today,
And tomorrow, until I no longer breathe.

It affords me active empathy.
For my community, my family, and friends,
And no dependence on an unseen deity,
To do it for me, so I might be selfish instead.

And if I am proven wrong by a deity,
Is it so wrong that I spent my life,
Spreading kindness as far as I can reach,
Instead of waiting for the deity to do it instead?

Cosmological Connection

Staring at the ceiling in the dark,
The universe pours from my crown.
There is no wall behind me,
Only the endlessness of existence.
I am so unfathomably small,
With relative meaninglessness,
In the grand scheme of the cosmos.
The tongue of universal deities is math.
It is how they express themselves to us,
And our mimicry is a poor substitution.
There is no point to our emotions,
Love will not stop entropy nor decay.
Perhaps the lack of utility and tangibility,
Signifies its own importance and gravity.
Ethereal love is feasibly the link,
That allows us to speak with divinity.

Coyotes III

In the dusk we silently stared at each other:
The coyote and the toddler.
Then I was stuffed into the cabin of a truck,
And our gaze was broken.

Sharing this, sitting with my professor,
He who walked the ancient lemon groves in Greece,
And listened with ears too large for his skull:
"I think it was reaching out to you."

In death, he has become dust.
I close my eyes and reach into the darkness,
The coyote was waiting for me.
We share our silence once more.

Corporate Coffee

Good morning worker!
Wait in line politely, please.
Make the order, hurry now!
Wait once more—be quiet cog.
Grab the cup and quaff it down.

It's full of deforestation,
Unethical business practices,
Single use plastics destined for landfills,
Abuse of the indigenous and death,
Pollutants pushed into our air, water, and earth.

Deliciously unsustainable.
Scald your throat, burn your skin,
Sue, get mocked, die in poverty,
Propaganda for status quo.
Drink in the capitalistic hellscape.

White People

I never understood my middle sister.
Or why she adopted a southern drawl,
When she had never left the valley.

But it must have been a new expression,
Of our people's tradition of taking,
From heritages that did not belong to them.

Learn to Love

Prick me and let me bleed on these sheets.
Take from me, because I don't know,
My value, or what love feels like.
Though I crave it.

Allow me to become addicted to touch,
And allow me to starve when you leave,
Unprepared for someone so hungry as I,
Though I will weep.

Push me over a table and off the road,
For my betrayal while you woo other women.
Let me run again, on taped-together bones,
Through pain I will grow.

Let this little dinghy toss me mercilessly,
As we cut through this sea, full of other fish.
Bruise me, tear me, cut me, suffocate me.
Though I will find my sea-legs,

Now, was that so hard? I ask myself.

Departure at Gate Seventeen

The cloying fingers of muck pulled my body.
Filled my soul with panic, binding my limbs,
As I drowned, my voice was locked in a box.
While my family watched on.

"You're fine. This is normal."
Gasping, painful lungs denied their words.
Tear stung eyes, agonized into silence.
I am buried in the layers in filth.

Straining fingertips tickle the air.
Is there light? Is that the sun?
Not the sun, the crimson glow of an exit.
It was not freedom, but it was better.

An Eye for an Eye

Thank you for thinking of me,
But I will return this gift I did not want,
And allow the negativity the flow,
Back into your waiting arms.

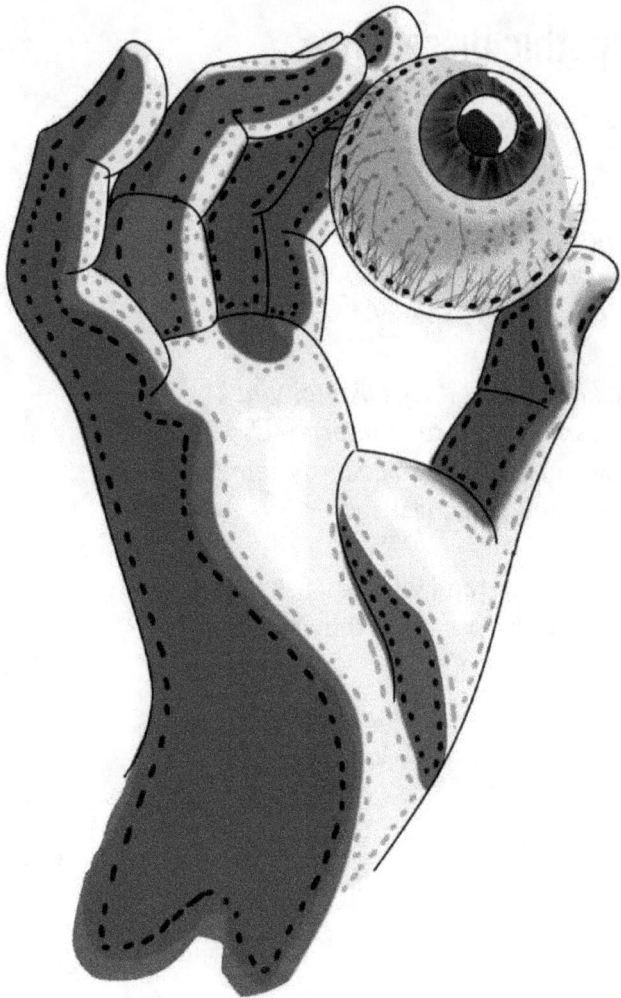

Empathic Dissonance

"The world is against us."
My father assured me.

"They never liked help, too proud."
"They would rather suffer, than admit weakness,"
She remembered sadly.

"We knew what it was like for you."
"It wasn't our place to interfere."
"How could you be so cold to them?"
They cooed and chastised.

I don't understand why you asked that.
These are the practices they taught me.

Bold of You

Bold of you to try,
To exceed the horrors,
Of my own mind.

I think you will find,
That you are quite out of your league,
When it comes to punishing me.

Time has honed my blade,
And exposed the weak points.
I am simply better at this than you.

Embrace the Cycle

Push me through the hole,
Where Ash and Embla were pulled.

And let the wolf-chased sun,
Dry my newly birthed skin.

Let that trickster steal my hair,
Until I am bald, save my golden crown.

I will spit in the pot with you,
And pour out refined wisdom.

We can wear our seal skins,
And wrestle on the beach for a jewel.

It is my delight and duty this cycle,
To drink within their hall.

Invitation

Let us burn the fire and waft the smoke.
Clean away the intrusive, and focus on the present,
As we welcome a new perspective.

Look into my eyes, ignore the shadows beyond.
Have we learned anything here?
Don't over think it, tell me what you feel.

Hold my cool hands though yours are feverish.
Suck in my exhalation to calm the palpitations.
Let me be your Virgil, watch your step.

You may feel cursed, but it is malicious healing—
Even swords must have impurities burned away.
Growth can only come from blessed pain.

It must be so.

Goodbye

Close my pages and lay me on the table.
Rest your eyes and soothe your heart.

Impossible person, who won't read this:
I know I have only screamed into the void.

Unheard, does not mean unsaid.
Greif is tumultuous and complex.

Slip me into your shelf, or nightstand,
Never to be seen again, no binding cracked.

Throw me into the rubbish—if you must
Hide me in the midden that you create.

What was said, remains said.
Rest now for a moment...

You have my consent to move on.

Illustrations

Art created by MJE Clubb in 2025 using the procreate application.

About the Author

MJE Clubb, lives in the Pacific Northwest with her husband, three teenagers, and a (probably) unreasonable number of pets.

Born and raised in the Willamette Valley, she spent her formative years on a farm in the river basin, surrounded by history accumulated through five generations.

As an adult, she spent her time in the service of her community serving at risk and vulnerable populations.

It is important to acknowledge that despite the longevity of her family's presence in Oregon, the homestead itself is the result of the Oregon Donation Land Claim Act. The land is on the traditional territory of Kalapuya Native American Tribes who were displaced by white settlers in the 1800s.

Other titles by MJE Clubb

Titles are available in paperback, hard cover, and for kindle.

<u>Novels</u>
Somewhere Long Forgotten (mystery)
Unwelcome (horror)
Blood and Water (fantasy)

<u>Short story collections</u>
Stray thoughts (horror)
Heartstrings (horror)
The Goddess Edda (creative mythology)

<u>Poetry collections</u>
An Estrangement of Humanity
Bitter Witch and Other Pet names

www.ingramcontent.com/pod-product-compliance
Lightning Source LLC
La Vergne TN
LVHW021404080426
835508LV00020B/2460